P9-DOC-105

EYES ON NATURE®
WILD CREATURES

Kidsbooks®

Copyright © 2010 Kidsbooks, LLC
3535 West Peterson Avenue
Chicago, Il 60659

All rights reserved, including the right
of reproduction in whole or in part in any form.

Eyes on Nature is a registered trademark of Kidsbooks, LLC.

Printed in China

061002002GD

Table of Contents

Written by
Rebecca L. Grambo
John Grassy
Robert Matero
Jane P. Resnick
and
Kerry Acker

Scientific Consultants

| Colleen M. McCann, Ph.D Wildlife Conservation Society | David Dickey Dept. of Herpetology American Museum of Natural History | MaryBeth Garriga The Raptor Center, St. Paul, MN | Paul Sweet American Museum of Natural History | Edward M. Spevak Wildlife Conservation Society, Bronx Zoo |

The bat is the only mammal that can fly.

MAMMALS EVERYWHERE

Mammals live in a wide variety of habitats. They walk the land, swim the seas, and even take to the air. You are one of them. Like tigers, whales, and bats, people are mammals.

BIG SPOTTED CATS ▼

Sometimes this animal is called a black panther. It is really a black leopard. You can see its spots. Instead of yellow with black spots, it is all black because its fur is colored by the pigment melanin (MELL-uh-nin). Melanin is the same pigment that gives our skin its unique color.

▲ FIRST HERE

Tiny insect-eaters that looked something like today's tree shrew (above) appeared about 195 million years ago in a world that belonged to the dinosaurs. These were the first mammals. Only about 65 million years ago, after most dinosaurs became extinct, did mammals begin to take on a wide variety of shapes and sizes.

TODAY'S COUNT

About 4,000 species of mammals exist today. The squirrel (below) and its rodent relatives make up the largest mammal group—in number of species and number of individual animals.

The African elephant ▶ is the largest living land mammal, weighing as much as eight tons.

BIG AND SMALL

Mammals come in a wide range of shapes and sizes—from the blue whale (below), more than 100 feet long and weighing 150 tons, to the pygmy shrew, which weighs only $7/100$ of an ounce.

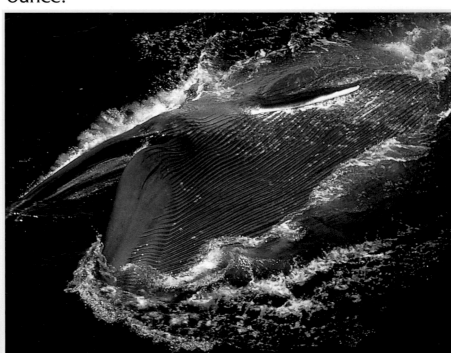

▲ LIVING ALL OVER

The red fox has the largest range of any carnivore (meat-eater) on Earth. This mammal lives on five continents and hunts in habitats ranging from the edge of the Sahara to the fringe of the northern tundra.

MAMMALS ARE...

All mammals have hair and are warm-blooded, breathe air, and nurse their young.

MILK FOR BABIES ▲

Female mammals, such as this saddleback sow, produce milk in their body to feed their offspring. Young mammals grow quickly on this fat-rich liquid diet.

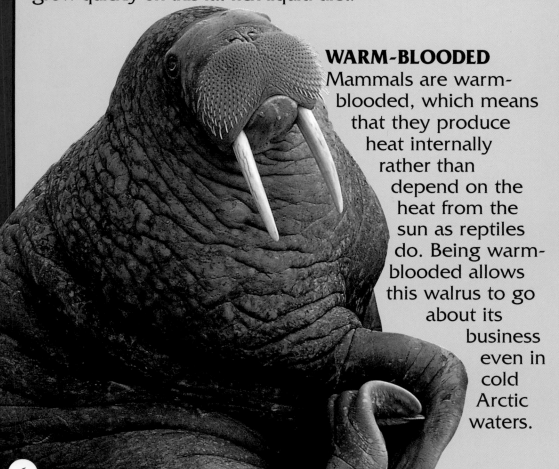

WARM-BLOODED

Mammals are warm-blooded, which means that they produce heat internally rather than depend on the heat from the sun as reptiles do. Being warm-blooded allows this walrus to go about its business even in cold Arctic waters.

YOU CAN'T SEE ME!

Deer fawns hide from danger by standing or lying very still. The white dots on their coat look like the spotty light coming through the trees or grass. In this field, a fawn's spots blend in very well with the clover blossoms around it.

BRAIN POWER▼

Some mammals are extremely intelligent and good at problem-solving. Dolphins learn easily and can remember complicated series of actions.

▼BEING BORN

Nearly all mammals give birth to live young. Some mammal babies can get around on their own immediately, but many are helpless and need lots of care. A joey, or baby kangaroo, is hairless and less than one inch long when born. It stays in its mother's pouch, nursing and growing, for six to eight months.

FAMILY TIES

Many mammals have strong family bonds. The relationship between mother and young is often especially close. In a pride of lions, cubs learn how to find food and watch for danger from their mother before going off on their own.

▼ The long claws of the three-toed sloth are perfect for clamping over tree branches, allowing the sloth to spend most of its life hanging upside down.

BODIES THAT WORK

Mammals have bodies to suit their lifestyles. Each species has developed specialized body parts for hunting or gathering food, defending itself, and traveling around in its environment.

TOUGH ▼ TEETH

The tiger and other meat-eaters have teeth that are good for holding prey and ripping flesh. Many rodents, such as the coypu (below, right) have large chisel-like front teeth designed for gnawing.

NIGHT EYES

Nocturnal mammals, such as this galago, have eyes that make the most of even the smallest amounts of light. A reflective layer at the rear of the eye bounces light back to the part of the eye where images are formed.

FINS AND FLIPPERS ▼

If you spend most of your life in the water, as this fur seal does, fins and flippers are more useful than arms and legs. Even on land, a fur seal's flippers work exceptionally well—a large fur seal can gallop faster than a human can run!

HORNS AND ANTLERS

Horns and antlers may be used for defense or in battles between males. Horns, like those of the bighorn sheep, last for the animal's life. They have a core of bone that is covered with keratin—the same material that makes up your fingernails. Antlers are also made of bone, but they do not last the animal's whole life. Each year in the winter, the antlers drop off, and a new set grows in the spring.

▼ A male elk, or moose, which grows as tall as 6 feet at the shoulders and weighs as much as 1,400 pounds, can have antlers that measure up to 5 feet across.

Rocky Mountain bighorn sheep

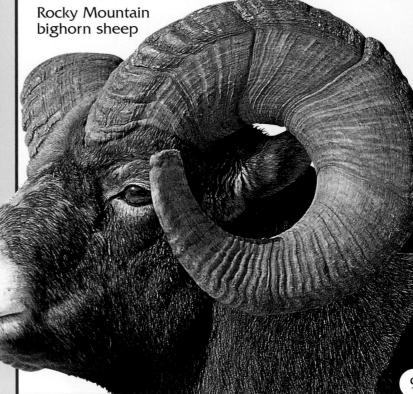

HANDY TAILS

When you are moving from branch to branch, trying to grab food and hang on at the same time, an extra hand is useful. Some tree-dwelling monkeys,

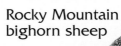

such as this spider monkey, have a strong tail, called a prehensile tail, which bends and can grasp things much the way a hand does.

FROM PLACE TO PLACE

Mammals have adapted to life in all kinds of places—on grassy plains and mountaintops, in desert sands and polar snows.

ON THE PLAINS

Flat, grassy plains are home to grazers, such as zebra (below), wildebeests, and impala. These grass-eaters are fast-moving, hoofed mammals that travel in herds for protection. Because they are prey for lions and other meat-eaters, grazers keep to their herd, especially at a water hole, where they are more likely to be attacked.

UP HIGH

The llama lives on the slopes of South America's Andes Mountains. Its blood has a lot of red blood cells, which are very efficient at collecting oxygen. This enables the llama to cope with the lower oxygen levels found at high altitudes.

UNDER GROUND ▲

The star-nosed mole spends its life underground, where smell may be the most important sense. Each of the 22 tentacles on its snout helps it locate prey in the dark.

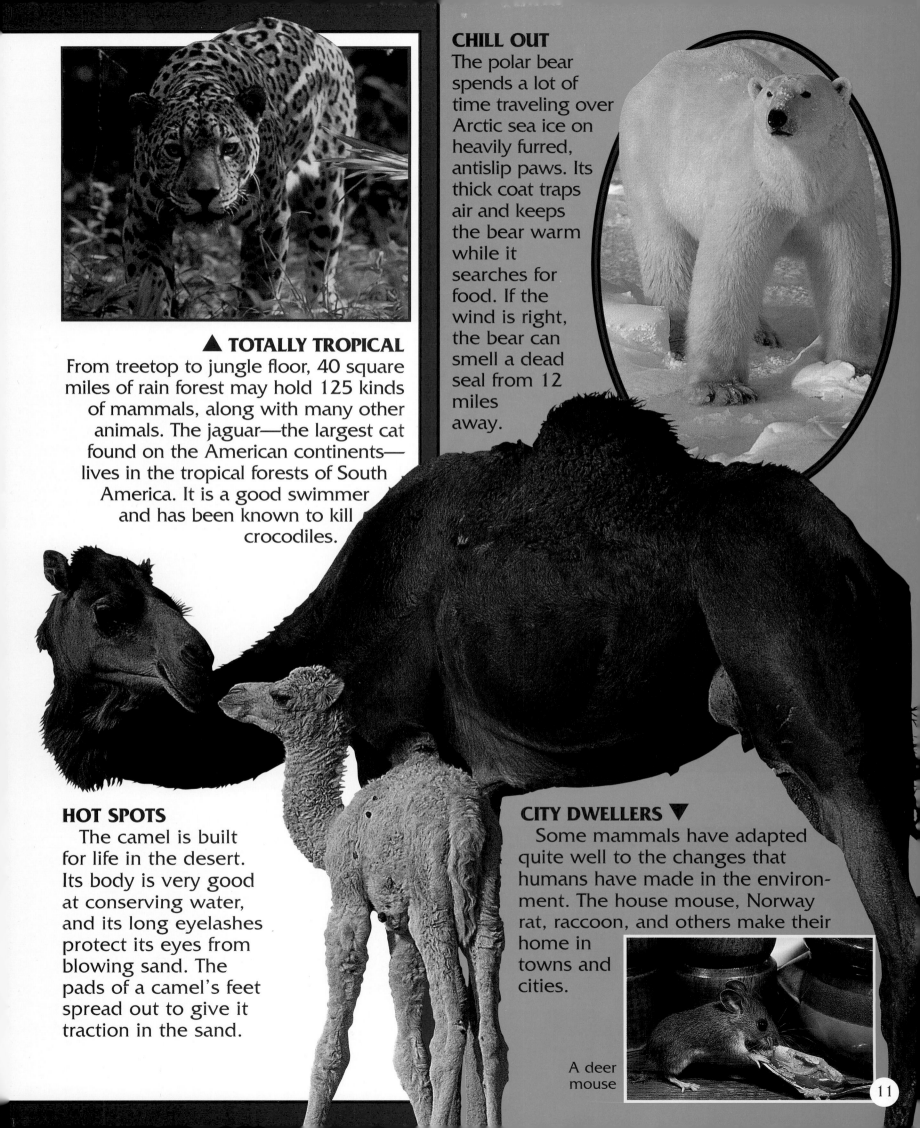

▲ TOTALLY TROPICAL

From treetop to jungle floor, 40 square miles of rain forest may hold 125 kinds of mammals, along with many other animals. The jaguar—the largest cat found on the American continents— lives in the tropical forests of South America. It is a good swimmer and has been known to kill crocodiles.

CHILL OUT

The polar bear spends a lot of time traveling over Arctic sea ice on heavily furred, antislip paws. Its thick coat traps air and keeps the bear warm while it searches for food. If the wind is right, the bear can smell a dead seal from 12 miles away.

HOT SPOTS

The camel is built for life in the desert. Its body is very good at conserving water, and its long eyelashes protect its eyes from blowing sand. The pads of a camel's feet spread out to give it traction in the sand.

CITY DWELLERS ▼

Some mammals have adapted quite well to the changes that humans have made in the environment. The house mouse, Norway rat, raccoon, and others make their home in towns and cities.

A deer mouse

THE WET ONES

Even though all mammals need to breathe air, many have evolved to spend life in or near water. Whales and dolphins never leave the sea and can stay underwater for hours at a time. To make breathing easier upon surfacing, they have developed nostrils called blowholes at the top of their head.

◀ **SEA UNICORN**
The 15-foot-long narwhal cruises the cold Arctic waters. In Europe during the Middle Ages, the narwhal's tusk, nearly 10 feet long, was believed to be the horn of the mythical unicorn. In fact, it is just an over-grown front tooth.

COOL TOOL
Webbed feet and a strong tail help the sea otter get around in the ocean. The otter sometimes places a flat rock on its chest and then pounds shellfish on it until the shellfish opens.

THINK PINK ▲
Largest of all river dolphins, the pink river dolphin of South America is about 7 1/2 feet long and weighs up to 280 pounds. Baby river dolphins are dark gray. As they grow older, their skin lightens so that blood vessels beneath the skin can be seen, which gives them a pink coloring.

12

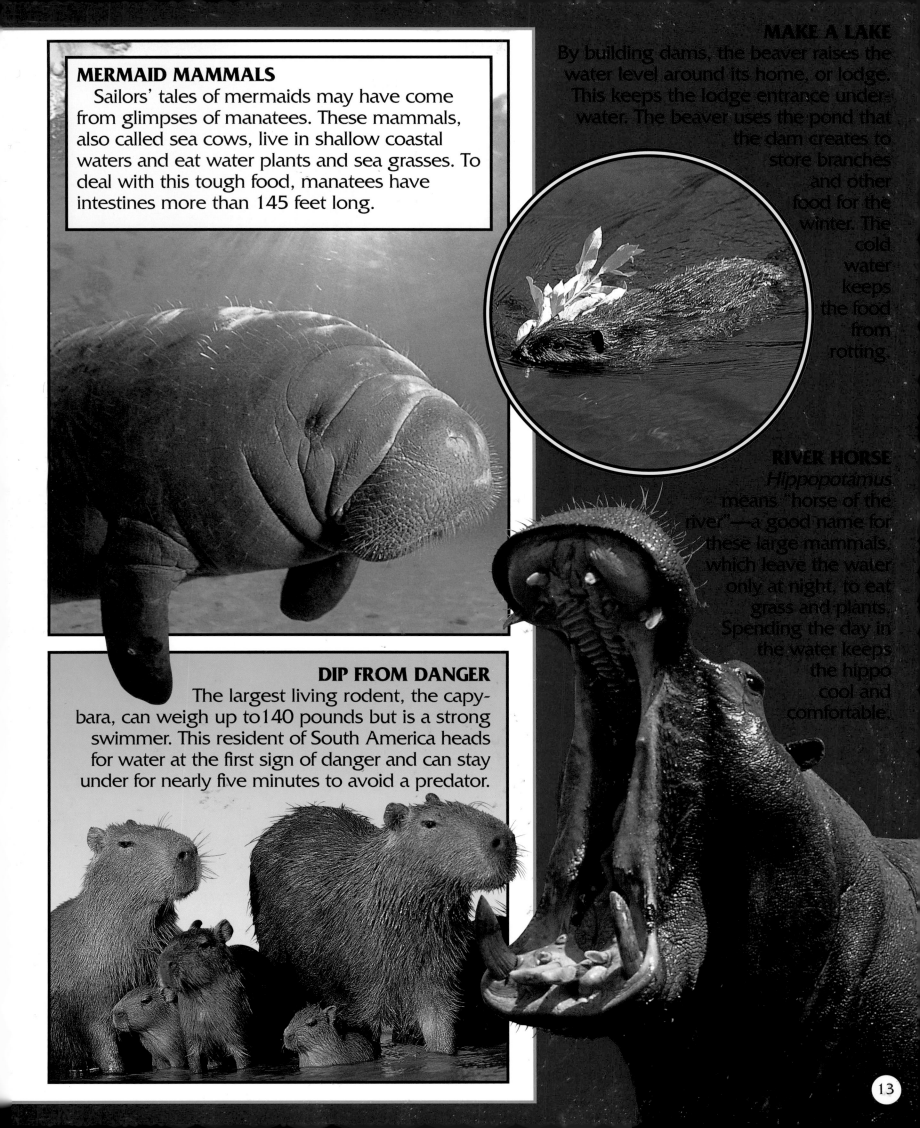

MERMAID MAMMALS

Sailors' tales of mermaids may have come from glimpses of manatees. These mammals, also called sea cows, live in shallow coastal waters and eat water plants and sea grasses. To deal with this tough food, manatees have intestines more than 145 feet long.

MAKE A LAKE

By building dams, the beaver raises the water level around its home, or lodge. This keeps the lodge entrance under water. The beaver uses the pond that the dam creates to store branches and other food for the winter. The cold water keeps the food from rotting.

RIVER HORSE

Hippopotamus means "horse of the river"—a good name for these large mammals, which leave the water only at night, to eat grass and plants. Spending the day in the water keeps the hippo cool and comfortable.

DIP FROM DANGER

The largest living rodent, the capybara, can weigh up to 140 pounds but is a strong swimmer. This resident of South America heads for water at the first sign of danger and can stay under for nearly five minutes to avoid a predator.

UNIQUE TREATS

As a group, mammals eat a varied diet, but some individual species have their own ideas about what foods are best.

MMM, ANTS

The anteater, a power-ful digger, tunnels into anthills and termite mounds in search of food. It eats insects with the help of its long, sticky tongue, while its tough skin protects it from bug bites.

LEAF EATER ▼

Thanks to its diet, the koala always smells a bit like cough drops. The koala mainly munches the leaves of just five or six kinds of eucalyptus, even though there are about 350 species from which to choose.

◄ FRUIT PLATE

The common palm civet is a catlike mammal that lives in hot, wet areas of Asia. A good climber, it spends much of its time in the trees looking for some of its favorite foods. The civet eats at least 35 kinds of fruit, including some that are poisonous to humans.

IT'S A STRAIN ▼

The humpback whale's favorite food is krill, which is only two to three inches long. The whale strains great mouthfuls of seawater through horny plates, called baleen, that hold back the shrimplike krill for the whale to swallow.

FISHY BEAR

Grizzlies gather along the Pacific Coast when salmon come up the rivers to spawn. They may feast on freshly caught fish or scavenge an easier meal of fish that are already dead.

CLEANING UP

Found throughout much of the Americas, the raccoon is known for ransacking garbage cans and scattering trash in residential communities. It also has a reputation for "washing" its food—exploring the object with its paws—even in the absence of water. The name *raccoon* comes from the Native American word *arakun*, which means "he who scratches with his hands."

ON THE HUNT

Predatory mammals catch their meals in many ways. The cheetah (below), accelerating like a sports car to speeds of up to 70 mph, must catch its prey quickly or give up. It is not built for endurance. Only about half of its chases end with a kill.

▼ TARGET IN SIGHT

Unlike members of the dog family, which rely heavily on their sense of smell to help them find prey, the cougar hunts mainly with its eyes. Once its prey is in sight, the cougar slowly stalks close enough to attack with a few bounding leaps.

PACK ATTACK

Wolves work as a pack to bring down their prey. A wolf pack, which may have 7 to 20 animals, is made up of several pairs of adults and some pups. Hunting as a group allows wolves to catch and kill bigger animals than a single wolf could handle.

WHALE OF A HUNTER

The orca, also known as the killer whale, is actually the largest of the dolphins. Orcas are fast, intelligent hunters that often work in a group. If they spot seals resting on ice floes, orcas may tip the ice, then catch the seals as they slide off. This orca has thrust itself close to shore to catch its meal.

TUNED IN ▼

Bats use a special kind of sense called *echolocation* to find prey. They send out high-pitched noises, which bounce off objects and return to the bat's ears. This sonar system allows bats to hunt at night for frogs, fish, and insects.

POISONOUS SPIT ▲

The water shrew swims through streams hunting for small fish, frogs, and crustaceans. When it catches them, a secret weapon helps the little shrew subdue struggling prey: Poisonous saliva flows down grooves in the shrew's teeth and into its prey.

◀ EATING SNAKE

The mongoose has a reputation for attacking even the largest and most poisonous snakes. Although the mongoose is not immune to a snake's venom, it is very quick and can avoid the lightning-fast strikes of a viper.

ON THE DEFENSE

Mammals use different tactics to avoid being eaten by predators. The snowshoe hare (right) has camouflage that changes with the seasons. In winter, the hare is white to blend in with the snow. In summer, its coat is brown to help it hide in grass and brush.

OUCH!

Porcupines keep their quill-filled rear ends pointed toward a potential attacker. The quills are so loosely attached to the porcupine's skin that even the slightest contact can leave a predator with a painful quill in its face or paw.

TURN AND FIGHT ▼

Weighing up to a ton, an angry Cape buffalo can discourage even the most determined predator. Cape buffalo have been known to charge and chase away attacking lions!

◄ **MAKE A STINK**

If a striped skunk stamps its front feet and does a handstand, step back and look out! A frightened or angry skunk can spray very smelly fluids, from glands near its tail, up to 10 feet away.

PLAY DEAD ▲
Some predators don't like to eat dead things. The opossum sometimes takes advantage of this by playing dead when a predator comes near. Once the danger has passed, the opossum hurries away.

ON GUARD
Meerkats live in family groups, and sometimes several families live together. Each day as the group forages for food, the meerkats take turns standing guard, watching for possible prey or danger.

FAMILY CIRCLE
When danger threatens, a herd of musk oxen forms a protective circle, with the calves in the center and the adults facing outward.

RUN FOR IT ▲
On the North American prairie, there are few places to hide. The pronghorn deer relies on its speed to carry it away from danger. It can run at 50 mph for almost a mile, and has been clocked running at 35 mph for more than three miles.

APES AND MONKEYS

Using its thumb and fingers, this woolly monkey grasps a tree limb.

HUMANLIKE?

How closely related are apes and monkeys to people? They, like us, belong to a group of mammals known as "primates." Primates share certain traits. We have thumbs that can grasp things, eyes positioned at the front of our head, and a large brain. Also, apes and monkeys, like people, have a social life.

▲ Great acrobats, these two orangutans hang tight for a kiss.

Apes and monkeys do wild things like beat their chest, swing from trees, and howl day and night. These highly advanced creatures also do much more. They show feelings of affection. They fight and make up. Some have even learned to use tools.

▼ MONKEY SEE...

Talk about smart! Apes and monkeys are very fast learners. A young female macaque discovered that dunking a sweet potato in the sea was the easiest way to clean sand off. In a short time, her family and friends, then the entire group, started washing their potatoes.

THE SPECIAL ONE

The tarsier is in a group by itself. To *primatologists,* the people who study primates, this creature has a strange mix of traits. It has the large eyes and ears of the prosimians. But it also has a short, furry nose like monkeys and apes.

WHAT'S A LEMUR? ▲

The lemur is a prosimian—a relative of apes and monkeys. Found only on the island of Madagascar, the ring-tailed lemur looks more like a cat than a monkey—with its whiskers and large ears.

WHAT A LIFE!

Compared to many animals, monkeys and apes live a long time. In the wild, monkeys can live for 20 years or more, and gorillas, chimpanzees, and orangutans may live past the age of 40.

21

MANY MONKEYS

The world has so many monkeys, about 130 species. Those that live in South and Central America are called New World monkeys, and those found in Africa and Southeast Asia are called Old World monkeys.

A langur from Asia ▶

BIG AND BAD ▼

The largest monkeys, baboons, have a tough character, which comes in handy around the lions and hyenas in Africa. Baboons spend the day on the ground, but sleep in trees or cliffs at night for safety.

LITTLE CRITTER ▼

The smallest New World monkey is the pygmy marmoset, just 5 inches long with an 8-inch tail. It lives in the rain forests of several South American countries. Like other New World monkeys, it spends most of its time in trees.

COLORFUL DIANA

The Diana monkey is a member of the guenon family, the most common group of monkeys in Africa. Guenons have long arms, legs, and tails, and brightly colored coats.

ABSOLUTE APES

The ape family has just four members: gibbons, chimpanzees, orangutans and gorillas; the last three are known as the "great apes" due to their size and body shapes. They live only in Africa and parts of Southeast Asia.

▲ High above the forest floor, 20 to 100 feet, orangutans spend much of their day swinging from limb to limb looking for food.

ACROBAT
Smallest of the apes, the gibbon has very long arms for its size, and uses them to swing through the trees. It can also walk along a branch using only its two legs, holding both arms out for balance.

APE OR ▲ MONKEY?
Besides their large size, apes are different from monkeys in other ways. They don't have a tail, and they "knuckle-walk" on their front hands. Monkeys scamper about on the flats of their palms, much like a squirrel.

SUPER SILVERBACK
Apes are big—really big. The largest and most powerful of all is the gorilla. A mature male "silverback" stands more than $5\frac{1}{2}$ feet tall and weighs an average of 350 pounds. Gorillas lead a quiet life, eating massive amounts of leaves, stems, bark, and roots.

LIVING ROOM

Apes and monkeys live in tropical forests and grasslands. They eat fruit, nuts, grass, leaves, insects, and other small animals.

The white-faced saki lives in South America's Amazon basin.

REAL SURVIVOR

In South Africa, the chacma baboon lives in deserts and plains, as well as along the rocky seashore, where it feeds on crustaceans. At night it sleeps on boulders or rocky cliffs.

▼ STAY AWAY!

Each group of apes and monkeys needs a place to call its own. White-handed gibbon families live in the forests of Southeast Asia, and they don't like trespassers. Each morning the male and female sing a duet for as long as 15 minutes, sending a message to other gibbons to stay away!

OUT ON A LIMB ▼

In the dense canopy of Brazil's rain forest, the golden lion tamarin eats, sleeps, and travels. To avoid predators, most forest-dwelling monkeys, such as tamarins and marmosets, sleep in the hollows of trees— a tough spot for a jaguar to reach.

SNOW MONKEY
The Japanese macaque has adapted to a harsh environment. On rugged Honshu Island, these monkeys endure snowy winters in the mountains. Once the trees have shed their leaves, the macaque gets through the cold season by feeding on bark.

MOUNTAINEER
In the forests of Africa, lowland and mountain gorillas live peacefully, having no natural enemy except people. Lowland and mountain gorillas look somewhat different. Western lowland gorillas have short, black fur and broad faces. Gorillas from the Eastern lowlands are the largest, and have long faces and short, black fur. Mountain gorillas, like the one shown here, have long, silky black fur and big jaws.

AMAZING BODY

Apes and monkeys are built for a life of climbing, grasping branches, and collecting food.

TALENTED TAIL

Like many other monkeys, the spider monkey can grasp a tree limb with its tail and hang safely while collecting fruit with both its hands.

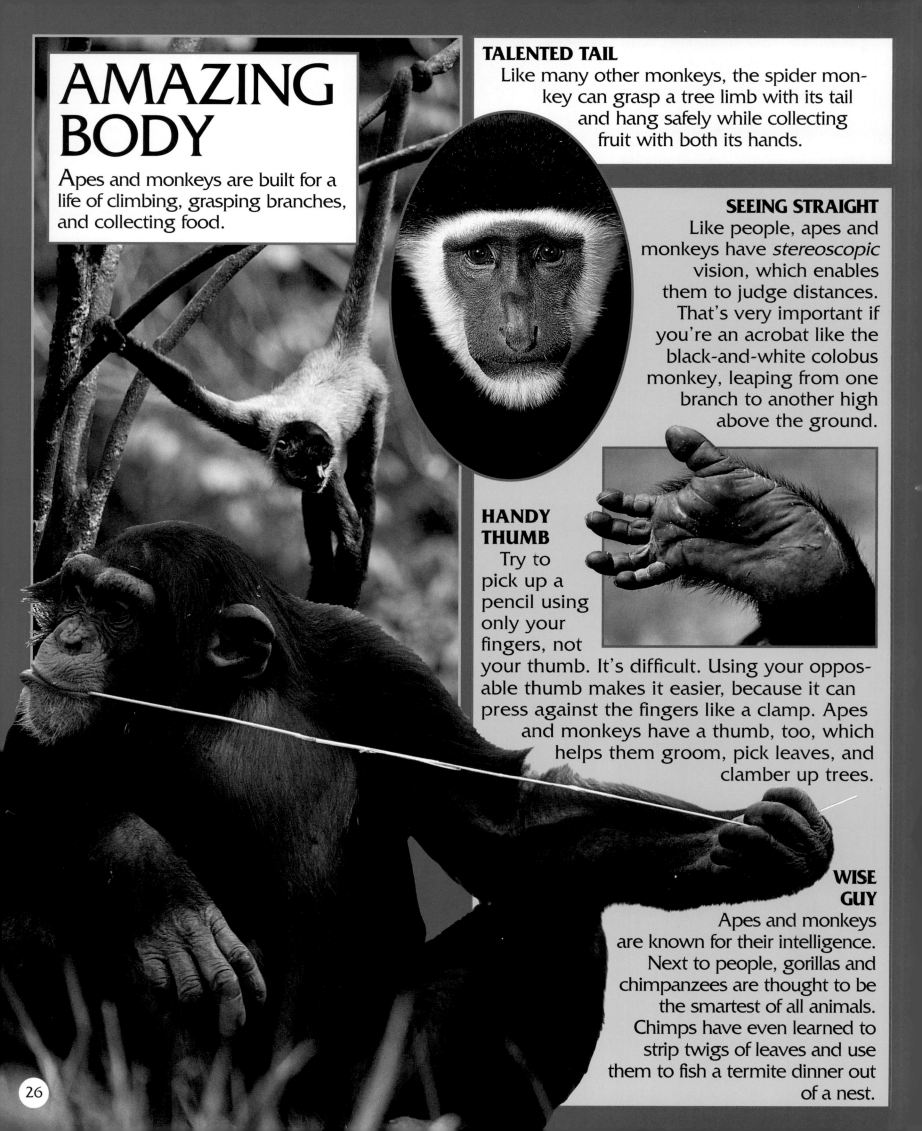

SEEING STRAIGHT

Like people, apes and monkeys have *stereoscopic* vision, which enables them to judge distances. That's very important if you're an acrobat like the black-and-white colobus monkey, leaping from one branch to another high above the ground.

HANDY THUMB

Try to pick up a pencil using only your fingers, not your thumb. It's difficult. Using your opposable thumb makes it easier, because it can press against the fingers like a clamp. Apes and monkeys have a thumb, too, which helps them groom, pick leaves, and clamber up trees.

WISE GUY

Apes and monkeys are known for their intelligence. Next to people, gorillas and chimpanzees are thought to be the smartest of all animals. Chimps have even learned to strip twigs of leaves and use them to fish a termite dinner out of a nest.

26

ON THE MOVE

Monkeys can really move through the trees, but the ape known as the gibbon is the champion swinger. It makes spectacular leaps from one tree to another, or it *brachiates* (BRAY-kee-ates) from limb to limb—using its long, powerful arms. It grabs a branch and swoops downward, then reaches with the other hand for another limb, and keeps on swinging!

PADDED SEAT

Old World monkeys, such as baboons, sleep sitting up, and they have a built-in cushion for comfort. Look on each side of the tail and you can see their two hairless pads of skin, called *ischial callosites*.

The hair of apes and monkeys offers protection from rain, wind, and biting insects. It often needs cleaning, and fellow troop members are eager to groom a friend.

IN THE CHEEK

Some monkeys have a special place for storing food—in cheek pouches! Baboons, macaques, and other monkeys stuff food into the pouches and snack on it later!

TALK ABOUT IT

Great communicators, apes and monkeys have many ways of warning each other of danger. And they have many ways of letting family or group members know what's on their mind.

Howler monkeys are known for their howl, which sounds a little like a dog's bark and can be heard up to two miles away.

LIP ACTION

Lip-smacking is used by monkeys as a friendly invitation for another monkey to approach. Goeldi's monkey opens and closes its mouth rapidly, and sometimes even sticks its tongue out!

CHIMP PALS

Friendships among chimpanzees are very strong and can last for years and years, even if one chimp should take up with another group. When two chimp friends meet after a period of separation, they throw their arms around each other, hug and kiss, and pat each other on the back.

ENEMY ALERT

The vervet monkey of Africa has developed specific alarm calls for each of the major predators it faces: eagles, leopards, and snakes. Group members will look up at the sky, run up a tree, or quickly climb even higher into the trees, depending on which predator is at hand.

PASS IT ON

When apes and monkeys think of a solution to a problem, the word gets around. One group of chimps that learned to use twigs to fish for carpenter ants passed on this technology to another community living some distance away.

TOUGH GUY

Baboons are tough characters, and the leader of the troop is the toughest of all. Feared and respected by his fellow baboons, the leader may only need to glare at an upstart male or a youngster causing too much mischief—and the problem is solved.

FANGS

Watch out for those teeth! Apes and monkeys have pretty sharp canines, which are sometimes used to threaten other troop members, or to defend against outsiders.

SWINGING BABIES

As mammals, the babies of apes and monkeys survive on their mother's milk. For warmth and protection, they cling to their mother until they are big enough to move about on their own.

AMAZON▶ TWINS

Most monkeys and apes give birth to a single infant. The marmosets of the Amazon are one of the few exceptions. They usually have twins.

HANG TIGHT ▲

Apes and monkeys are always on the move, and there's no time to stop for a struggling infant. Mothers go about their regular business—climbing, hanging, leaping from one limb to another—all with baby on board.

SHOW OF COLOR

Babies need special care. One way to get it is to look really different from the adults—by being bright orange! In contrast to its gray relatives, this colorful silver leaf monkey seems to "scream" for everyone's attention. But in adulthood it, too, will grow gray fur.

PLAYTIME

Playing games and goofing off is as much fun for young apes and monkeys as it is for you. During play, youngsters make friendships that can last throughout their life. Playing also helps young monkeys learn the rules of the group.

▼ Wrestling on a limb develops the muscles and reflexes of these two young Japanese macaques.

▲ For a young proboscis monkey, playing with a fat tail is just as much fun as climbing a tree.

ALL GROWN UP ▲

Male mountain gorillas acquire the silver hair on their back around age 10. At this point they must leave the group. They may live alone for a while, but will gradually find female gorillas from other groups to join them and help start their own troop.

TAKING CARE

Many monkey and ape dads protect their family. But caring for babies often falls to the female. Among langurs, females gather around a new baby, as if asking the mother for a chance to hold it. The mother lets them, but if danger approaches, she grabs the baby and dashes up a tree.

What does it take to set a monkey apart from the others? Maybe an extraordinary nose or a colorful face? If so, these monkeys take the prize.

LONG LEGS ▼
Reaching speeds of 35 miles per hour, the patas monkey is the fastest around, and long legs are part of its secret. Because it stays mostly on the ground, ranging the plains of Africa with hyenas and leopards, its speed is a much needed defense.

◀ **BIG-EYED**
The night monkey, with its very large round eyes, is the only monkey in the world that is *nocturnal,* or active at night. Found in Central and South America, night monkeys feed on fruit and leaves, and sleep in hollow trees during the day. Not surprisingly, they are also called owl monkeys.

BATHING BEAUTIES
Monkeys taking a bath? Not exactly. In the cold, snowy mountains of Japan, these macaques sit in hot springs just to get warm.

NOSEY GUY

With his large fleshy nose, the male *proboscis* (meaning nose) monkey got his name fair and square. These monkeys are found only on the island of Borneo, Malaysia, where they live in swamp forests and along creeks near the sea. They are good swimmers, and can even swim underwater.

COLOR COUNTS ▼

A male mandrill has bright blue cheeks and a red nose, which brightens when he is challenged. If that isn't enough to discourage outsiders, he has very sharp canines, four inches long!

◄ LIP FLIP

Geladas are large monkeys with a patch of naked, pink skin on their chest. These baboons have a strange-looking way of baring their teeth and gums. They flip back their lip!

◄ BLUSHER

The uakari (wah-CAR-ee), has a red face and bald head! It's an amazingly expressive monkey. When really angry or excited, its face turns even brighter. If it feels threatened, it shakes the branches and makes a noise that sounds like laughter.

INCREDIBLE CHIMPS

Chimps are so inventive, they've been known to make their own "shoes"—using twigs as sandals to protect their feet from thorns! They also use rocks to crack open nuts, eat bitter plants to cure stomachaches, and hunt in organized groups.

ALL SIZED UP

Stand next to a common adult male chimp and you'll find he's not very small. He may reach 5 feet in height and weigh as much as 170 pounds. A second species, known as bonobos, are almost the same size. They live in the rain forests of Zaire, whereas the common chimp ranges the forests and savannas of western and central Africa.

HANG ON, KID

Getting around means hanging on to mother. Baby chimps cling to their mother as soon as they're born and stay close to her for about five years. Wherever she goes, the baby chimp is aboard for the ride.

WHAT A HOOT

With up to 120 members living in their group, chimps have to communicate. When they find food, they hoot, scream, and slap logs. Even young chimps can make as many as 32 different sounds.

REAL PERSONALITY

Can you tell one chimp from another? Next time you go to the zoo, spend some time with these primates. Their face, voice, walk, and personality are so different from one another that it takes primatologists just a few days to easily distinguish 20 or more chimps.

EXPRESS YOURSELF

On seeing a waterfall, one group of chimpanzees performed a dance, as if awed by the water. Chimps say a lot with their body, especially their face. They pout when they surrender to an attacker, and grin when excited or afraid. They can also look thoughtful or disbelieving.

BIG DIET

At one time, people thought chimps were strictly plant eaters. But primatologist Jane Goodall discovered that chimps on occasion also eat meat, such as monkeys, pigs, birds, and antelopes. They may eat a quarter-pound of meat in one day when hunting.

FIERCE FIGHTS

We usually think of chimpanzees as fun-loving and silly. But fights among male chimps over leadership can result in serious injuries. In one population, neighboring bands of chimpanzees were even observed waging deadly war.

This young chimp has only fun in mind! ▶

35

ORANGUTANS

Found only in portions of Borneo and Sumatra, this reddish-brown ape is known as the orangutan, or "person of the forest." The name suits it because an orangutan hardly ever comes out of the trees, living as much as 100 feet above the forest floor.

FRUIT LOVERS

The orangutan, who spends more than half the day eating, is the largest fruit-eating animal in the world. In the tropical forests, different kinds of fruit become ripe at different times of the year. The orangutan eats figs, mangoes, and its favorite fruit—the large, prickly durian. When fruit can't be found, the orangutan dines on leaves and bark.

NOTABLE LIPS

Orangutan lips come in handy when both hands and feet are needed to travel. Opened wide, they can hold a large piece of fruit. Orangutans also use their lips to feel the fruit, puckering up and touching them to the surface.

SHOUT IT OUT

A male orangutan's territory is about two square miles, and he shouts a clear warning to protect it. His morning "long call" is a series of roars and groans that can go on for nearly five minutes. Even in the dense growth of the rain forest, the call is heard by other orangutans as far as a mile away.

WILD LOOKS

Orangutans have some pretty wild looks— with arms one and a half times longer than their legs. And they are not so small. The males are about 5 feet tall and 220 pounds. The females are about half as heavy.

◀ With age, the male orangutan develops large cheek and chest pouches which frame his face.

ESCAPE ARTIST

There is no doubt that orangutans are smart. In zoos, they're known as escape artists. An orangutan named Bob broke out of three different cages at the San Diego Zoo, including one that had successfully held lions and grizzly bears.

LONERS

The orangutan is the most unsociable of all apes and monkeys. Male orangutans are loners. After mating with a female, they return to their solitary life. Mothers will sometimes feed and travel with other females and their young, but only for a short time. Baby orangutans stay with their mom for about six years.

ACROBATIC

Orangutans are great acrobats. Their strong arms, which span eight feet, really get them around. They prefer to travel by swinging rather than come down from their tree and walk. In fact, down on the ground orangutans are quite clumsy.

THE GREATEST APE

When early European explorers came back from Africa, they told fantastic stories about the gorilla's enormous size and savage temper. African gorillas are huge, but they are also very shy and peaceful. Their only natural enemies are people.

LAID BACK

Gorillas take it easy. They only travel about 400 yards per day. The group gets up at dawn to begin feeding, then moves into their nest of leaves and grasses for the afternoon, where adults relax and groom, and youngsters play. In late afternoon they rise to feed again, but by sunset are back in their nest for the night.

SHOW OFF ▼

When two gorilla groups meet, things can be tense. The dominant male silverbacks may put on elaborate, lengthy displays to intimidate one another—glaring, hooting, chest-beating, and standing on two legs. Each leader is concerned about protecting his troop.

THE BOSS

It's an awesome sight when a male silverback stands upright and begins hooting and chest-beating. His actions mean different things depending on the situation. He may be warning his group of danger or telling a male intruder he is not welcome.

◀ A COOL DRINK

Gorillas feed heavily on succulent (water-holding) plants such as wild celery. Since these plants are so rich in water, gorillas seldom have need for drinking water in the wild. A thirsty gorilla can also usually find a leaf with rain or condensation on it, and lick off the water.

SMART TALKER ▼

Apes are great communicators. One famous gorilla named Koko, who lives at The Gorilla Foundation, has even learned to use more than 500 words in American Sign Language. For her twenty-fifth birthday, Koko asked for a box of "scary" rubber snakes and lizards!

▲ A female's closest relationships are with the silverback and her babies.

NOSE PRINTS

Like human fingerprints, each gorilla has a unique nose print—the lines above the nostrils. The flare or shape of a gorilla's nostrils are also unique. Researchers use these visual marks to identify each gorilla in a group.

REMARKABLE REPTILES

Millions of years ago reptiles dominated the land, sea, and sky. Most of these ancient reptiles—including the dinosaurs—suddenly died out about 65 million years ago. No one knows exactly why. However, five different groups of their ancestors—snakes, crocodilians, lizards, turtles and tortoises, and the tuatara—about 6,500 different species in all, adapted to the changing world and survive today on every continent except Antarctica.

Sun Seekers

Reptiles have thick, scaly skin which prevents their bodies from drying out. The scales are made from keratin, the same material found in your fingernails and hair. The body temperature of these cold-blooded creatures depends on their surroundings. It goes up in warm weather and down in cold weather.

The heat from the sun warms the blood of this basking crocodile.

Shedding Skins

Most reptiles keep growing throughout their lives. Snakes and some lizards are able to shed their scaly outer layer of skin as they outgrow it. Lizard skin falls off in flakes but snakes shed their entire skin — sometimes unbroken—at one time.

Lots of Lizards

Lizards come in many sizes and colors, and some, like Jackson's chameleon, even have horns! A chameleon's eyes move independently of each other and in any direction. This allows it to search for food and avoid being eaten at the same time.

Turtles, crocodilians, and most snakes and lizards are hatched from eggs. Reptiles build nests of rotting plant material or dig holes in the warm sand or soil where they deposit their eggs. Some snakes and lizards are born live from eggs that hatch in their mother's body.

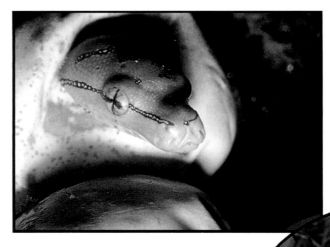

When they are ready to hatch, baby reptiles use a special pointed egg tooth or spike located on their snouts to chisel through the shell. Soon after, the egg tooth falls off. The hatchlings are identical to their parents—only smaller.

The Ancient One ▼
Lizard-like in appearance, the tuatara can trace its ancestors back to the time before dinosaurs roamed the Earth. The only survivors of this ancient group of reptiles live on a few islands near New Zealand.

Life In A Shell
The turtle's hard protective shell has enabled it to survive on Earth for over 250 million years. However, some sea turtles have developed a smoother, lighter, more streamlined shell, helping them to better adapt to life in the ocean.

TORTOISES AND TURTLES

Giant Tortoise

About 250 species of turtles and tortoises—the only reptiles with shells—inhabit the warmer areas of the Earth. The turtle's shell system has protected it so well that turtles have lived on Earth, practically unchanged, for about 200 million years.

When this painted turtle feels threatened, it tucks itself into its "home" until the danger passes. ▼

Diamondback Terrapin

Green Sea Turtle

What's in a name?
The name turtle usually refers to animals that live in freshwater—lakes, rivers, ponds, and streams. Sea turtles live in the ocean. Turtles that spend most or all of their time on land are called tortoises. Terrapin, a native American word meaning "little turtle," refers to small freshwater turtles, in particular the diamondback terrapin.

Carapace

Plastron

◄ Either a layer of tough leathery skin, or hard plates called scutes [scoots] cover the shell. Each species has its own scute pattern which keeps getting larger as the turtle grows.

Scute Pattern

Shell System
The turtle's shell is part of its skeleton. The shell is made up of two parts, the curved upper part (carapace) and the flattish lower part (plastron).

Clever and Deadly

Although toothless, this American snapping turtle is ready to use its strong, sharp beak to deliver a vicious bite. The snapper prefers to live in quiet muddy streams and ponds where it can snap away at fish, frogs, and water birds.

The alligator snapping turtle lies camouflaged in the mud with its mouth open. The turtle wriggles a worm-like pink flap on its tongue to lure small fish inside its deadly jaws.

Instead of teeth, turtles have beak-like jaws which snap and chop plants and small animals into bite-sized pieces. On land, turtles feed mainly on slow-moving prey, such as insects and worms. Many eat plants, too. Tortoises are vegetarians.

Loose fringes of skin dangle from the neck and head of the South American matamata turtle. Mistaking the fringes for worms, fish are lured close to its jaws. Suddenly, the strange-looking matamata opens wide and sucks in its dinner!

43

BIRDS THAT PREY

Birds of prey are meat-eating birds that use their strong feet to catch and kill prey. They also have strong, hooked beaks for tearing into flesh. Birds of prey are sometimes called raptors.

The bald eagle.

SHE'S BIGGER
Unusual among birds, raptor females are generally bigger than males. In some species, such as the little sparrowhawk (left), the female may be twice as big. Other raptors show less difference. Among species of vultures, males and females are about the same size.

DAY AND NIGHT ►
Most birds of prey are diurnal—active during the day. Most owls, however, are nocturnal. They do their hunting at night, relying on their hearing and low-light vision to locate prey.

SIMPLY BIRDS
Many birds, like the heron at right, eat other animals. But they are not called birds of prey, because they do not have the same kind of body or hunting methods that eagles, hawks, and other birds of prey do.

BIG AND ▲ LITTLE

Raptors come in all sizes. Biggest of them all, the Andean condor (above) may weigh 25 pounds and have wings stretching to over 10 feet. It's about 250 times heavier than the smallest bird of prey, the tiny Asian falconet.

TOP OF THE HEAP

Raptors, such as this martial eagle, sit at the top of the food chain. Much like a lion, they hunt other animals, but almost nothing else hunts them. Their only enemies are other birds of prey and humans.

WEAK FEET

Vultures, such as this white-backed vulture, are considered birds of prey even though their feet are weak. Because vultures feed mainly on carrion (dead animals), lacking grasping power is not a big problem for them. Their beaks do all the work!

A HUNTER'S BODY

Birds of prey have a body suited for hunting other animals. From beak to tail feathers, every part serves a purpose.

A peregrine falcon.

▼FINE FEATHERS

Feathers do many jobs for birds of prey. Soft down keeps the birds warm. Strong feathers on the wings allow the birds to control flight. Tail feathers are used for steering and braking. The flight feathers on the wings of many owls, including this great horned owl, have a soft edge that makes flight noiseless.

TALONS OF DOOM▼

If you were a bird of prey, your toenails would be talons. A raptor's talon-tipped feet are its most important weapon. Some fish-eating raptors, such as this osprey, have specially curved claws and spiny bumps on their feet to help them hook and hang on to their wriggling catch.

▲NO CHEWING

Raptors, such as this Steller's sea eagle, have a big, strong beak that is great for tearing meat. But they don't have heavy teeth and jaws for chewing, because that would weigh them down. They do their chewing inside a part of the stomach called the gizzard. The gizzard's strong muscles contract around the food, grinding it against the rough inner surface to break it down.

WONDER WINGS▼

Raptors that spend lots of time soaring have long, broad wings. By catching rising air currents, a bird like the turkey vulture (below) can cruise for hours and barely flap its wings. Soaring saves a lot of energy. Falcons, on the other hand, are fast-flapping flyers. Their narrow, pointed wings enable them to maneuver easily.

LIGHT BONES

To be able to fly well, birds of prey must weigh as little as possible. Hollow, air-filled bones are light but strong. Raptor skeletons are so light that in some species, such as the bald eagle, the bird's feathers weigh more than its bones!

EYE MOVEMENT

Raptor eyes are so big that they cannot move in their socket. The bird has to turn its whole head to look around. Raptors rely on their eyes and must avoid injuring them. A bony ridge above the eye gives some protection. Raptors also have a tough, partly transparent third eyelid that closes over their eyes to protect them when the birds are attacking prey or flying through branches.

EAGLE EYES

Birds of prey have eyesight that is at least two to three times better than ours. Some can see a grasshopper from a hundred yards away—the length of a football field! Eagles, such as the golden eagle (right), can spy rabbits and other prey from over a mile away.

PENGUINS

Will the real penguin please stand up? There are 17 species of penguins, and no two are exactly alike. Some have orange head tufts that look like crazy eye-brows. Some have brushy tails. Some are aggressive. Others are mild-mannered.

An Emperor Penguin and chick

HEAVYWEIGHTS

Three-and-a-half feet and over 60 pounds is a lot of bird. That's the Emperor, the largest of all. The King Penguin is the next heaviest at about 35 pounds. With lovely orange or yellow patches around their ears, and brilliant orange around their neck, the Kings are very handsome birds.

The King Penguin

PINT-SIZED PENGUIN

The shy Little Penguin is so delicate, it has been called the Fairy Penguin. It grows to only a foot-and-a-half, weighs under three pounds, and is the smallest of all penguins.

FEATHERED FRIENDS

The Macaroni Penguin has a "crest" of orange and yellow feathers. It gets its name from a fancy hairstyle that was popular among young men in England during the late 18th and early 19th centuries.

LOUDMOUTH

The Chinstrap is one of the brush-tailed penguins, which have long tails that sweep behind them. The Chinstrap stands a little over two feet tall and has a black stripe across its chin. It also has an ear-splitting call.

DONKEY CALL

A penguin that looks like it's been standing in the mud is the Black-footed Penguin. Its less-lovely name is the Jackass Penguin because it makes a loud braying noise like a donkey.

YELLOW-EYED

The Yellow-eyed is one of the tallest penguins. A bit different from the black-and-white variety of penguins, the Yellow-eyed has a slate-blue back, white undersides, and striking yellow eyes.

JUMPING GENTOO

A white band that goes from eye to eye is the mark of the Gentoo Penguin. This 14-pound bird, sometimes called the Johnny Penguin, runs, jumps, and even slides on its belly on sand.

BOLD LIVING

Penguins live only below the equator. Some come ashore on Antarctica, frigid home of the South Pole. But others do not live in cold places. They are found on the coasts and islands of South America, Africa, Australia, and New Zealand.

These ▶ Emperor Penguins enjoy the ease of ice travel in Antarctica.

ICE ISLAND

Antarctica, covered by a sheet of ice nearly a mile thick, is one of the coldest places on Earth. This continent is the breeding ground of the Adélie, Emperor, Chinstrap, and Gentoo penguins. But the Emperor is the only penguin that spends the winter there.

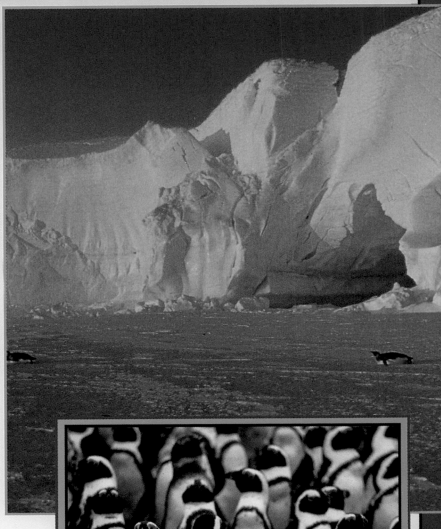

Adélies in a snowstorm.

▲ BIRD WATCHING

The first time Europeans set eyes on a penguin was when explorer Vasco da Gama sailed down the coast of Africa in 1499. One surprised sailor reported that he saw birds that made a sound like a mule and couldn't fly. Almost 500 years later, the Black-footed Penguin is still there, living on the coasts and small islands around the southern tip of Africa.

HOMEBODIES ▼

The coasts of New Zealand, Australia, and some surrounding islands are the homes of Little Penguins. These birds don't migrate like some other penguins. They travel only between their nest and the sea, about a third of a mile. It's a short but risky trip, threatened by the likes of cats, dogs, weasels, and even cars.

HOT AND COLD

Galapagos Penguins make their nests on the Galapagos Islands, off the coast of South America. That's nearly on the equator, a very hot spot! But the ocean there is cold, fed by a current flowing from the icy Antarctic— and filled with the foods that penguins like to eat.

NAMESAKE ▼

Magellanic Penguins have a name from the history books. When Ferdinand Magellan, the Portuguese explorer, led the first expedition around the world in 1519, he sailed around the tip of South America. That's where the Magellanics live, on both the Pacific and Atlantic coasts.

▼ Galapagos Penguins share their home with another ocean-goer— the marine iguana.

WARM BODIES

Penguins are warm-blooded creatures, just like people. Their normal body temperature is 100 to 102°F. Ours is 98.6°F. How do they stay warm in icy waters? Layers of insulation. Under their skin they have fat, known as blubber. Covering the skin are fluffy feathers, called *down,* and a tightly packed layer of outer feathers, which seals in warmth.

CUDDLE HUDDLE ▲

Emperor Penguins have the coldest breeding grounds—in Antarctica. They incubate their eggs in extreme weather, standing motionless on the ice. Sometimes one body just doesn't create enough heat. So they form a tight huddle. That's as many as 6,000 penguins squeezing shoulder to shoulder!

◀ BONE BONUS

Normally, birds have light, hollow bones that make flight easier. But penguins have heavy, solid bones that suit their way of life in the water. The weight lets them get their body underwater—where they can use their powerful flippers to swim.

SUPER FEET

There's more to penguins than feathers. Look at their feet. On land, penguins can walk, run, and hop. At sea, they use their webbed feet as rudders for steering.

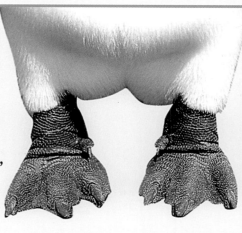

◀ FEATHER CARE ▶

A penguin's feathers are slick and dense. One square inch of penguin is covered with about 70 feathers, all overlapping like fish scales or shingles on a roof. Penguins *preen* their feathers, applying oil from an oil gland. The overlapping feathers and the oil create a waterproof, windproof suit.

◀ Two bills are better than one, so these Macaroni Penguins seem to think.

This ▶ Gentoo gets its feathers ready for the water by preening.

COLOR COATED

Color counts when a penguin is trying to keep warm. Black absorbs heat, and white reflects heat. A chilly penguin turns its black back to the sun and absorbs the warmth. A penguin in danger of overheating turns its white chest to the sun to reflect light.

▼ AIR WAYS

Too hot or too cold, both are problems for penguins. In warm places, such as the Galapagos Islands, penguins need to cool off. Feather fluffing is the answer. Penguins can lift their feathers and keep them up, so air can cool their skin. They also stick out their winglike flippers to help heat escape.

MADE TO MOLT ▼

Feathers don't last forever. Most birds replace them by *molting,* shedding old feathers and growing new ones. But penguins need their feathers in the icy sea. They molt all at once, and during that time—as long as a month—they stay out of the water.

This Galapagos Penguin stretches out its flippers to cool off.

THE MATING GAME

In the mating season, all penguins head for land. Each species has its own territory, and some are very far from their ocean homes. The Adélies nest in the spring, which begins in October in Antarctica. But the land is still surrounded by sea ice. To reach their rookery, the penguins trudge across the ice—for as much as 60 miles! ▶

◀ CHILLY WINTER

Emperor Penguins start breeding in the winter, which begins in March. There is no sun at that time. The penguins stay on the grim ice for six months, until their chicks are ready to be on their own when summer arrives.

SHOW-OFFS ▶

A male penguin has a walk that gets females to follow him. It's called a "display" or "advertisement walk." The King Penguin, with his spectacular orange neck markings, is the best on the block. He struts and turns his head from side to side so the female can see just how handsome he is.

LOVE CALL

There is high drama in the rookeries when mating begins. Each male must attract a female, and they do it by "calling." They stand with their back arched, head raised, and wings outstretched, and raise a wild trumpeting cry.

TUNE FOR TWO

All penguin pairs "sing" a duet as part of their display, and it's not just for entertainment. They learn to recognize each other's voice. That's very important because there are thousands of look-alikes in a rookery.

▼ YOU'RE MINE!

When a male and female become a pair, they cement the bond in a "mutual display." The two penguins, depending on the species, may raise their heads, touch necks, vibrate their flippers, or slap each other on the back.

PENGUIN PAIRS

Most penguins stick to the same partner. One theory for this behavior is that most return to their old territory and meet up automatically. But some scientists believe that penguins recognize each other by voice and sight, even after a year.

NEST, SWEET NEST

To build a nest, to find a mate, and to breed—that is the life's work of a penguin. All species are similar in these activities, but they are different, too. Just look at their nests!

▲ GHOSTLY GROUND

On the eastern coast of Argentina, there is an eerie noise that comes from holes in the ground, inspiring legends of ghosts and even devils. The sound comes from penguins—thousands of Magellanics, whose dug-in burrows form huge underground cities.

Black-footed Penguins dig burrows, too, ▶ but will also build nests above ground, using vegetation, feathers, or stones.

A Rockhopper and its egg.

BOUNCING BIRDS

Rockhoppers build nests on steep rocky areas. They get there by jumping. With both feet held together, they bounce four to five feet from one ledge to another. Macaroni Penguins build their nests on steep, rough ground, too. Sometimes they build on lava flows, rock slopes, and in caves.

▲ Nesting Macaroni mates.

PRECIOUS STONES ▶

Stones are valuable to Adélies. Stones are the only material they have with which to build their nests in Antarctica. Sometimes the right-sized rocks are in short supply. So every Adélie watches its stones, or a neighbor will steal them!

◀ MALE DUTY

As soon as eggs are laid, the female heads for the sea to find food. The male stays with the eggs. By the time the Adélie female returns, the males haven't eaten for about two weeks. Then it's his turn to eat while she stays with the eggs.

TAKING TURNS ▶

Gentoos hollow a nest in the ground and line it with grass. Then the male and female take turns keeping the egg warm against their *brood patch,* a featherless area on the belly.

FOOTHOLD

King Penguins have a territory rather than a nest. They incubate an egg standing up, and the spot where they stand is theirs. The sea is close to their colony, so parents eat and return often.

LIVING TOGETHER

Gather thousands of penguins together and what have you got? A rookery. Large rookeries can cover miles. But each pair of penguins gets only about one square yard of space to build a nest. It's crowded and noisy, but it's home.

▼ VOICES CARRY

Penguins get along in these huge throngs by "calling"—a cross between trumpets blaring and donkeys braying. Each species has its own unique call. Each penguin has its own particular sound. And they locate one another by voice. Shouting, they let each other know to "watch out" or "stay clear!"

In a rookery, it gets really crowded!

◄ King Penguins communicating.

◀ BODY LANGUAGE

Penguins communicate by gesture as well as by voice. They bump, paddle, and peck. They stare, bow, and crouch. Through sound and movement, they let others know their situation. They are male or female. They need a mate or don't. They want a nest or have one. They like each other or not.

SAFE CIRCLE ▼

For almost all animals, there is safety in numbers, especially when it comes to the young. When chicks are strong enough, both parents head for the sea. The chicks group together in a *creche*, or nursery, where they're less likely to be attacked by predators.

▼ Emperor chicks have to huddle to keep warm.

MA! IT'S ME! ▶

Ever get lost? Imagine looking for your parents among millions of others! But in the penguin world, chicks and parents recognize each other's calls and always find one another. Even while the chick is breaking out of its egg, it is calling so its parent will get to know its voice.

BACKYARD VISITORS

There's a zoo on the loose just outside your door! Backyard animals play, eat, sleep, preen, prowl after one another, and raise their babies. To see all this happen, you need only to open your eyes to nature.

LOOKING AT YOU

Have you ever heard a grasshopper making music, or seen a bird pause on a branch with a bug in its beak? Animals can see, hear, and smell *you,* too. If you want to observe them, you must be nearly invisible, or they may run away. Wear clothes that aren't too bright, hide behind trees, stay downwind, and, most of all, be quiet.

DO NOT DISTURB

Imagine someone tearing down the walls of your room and carrying your possessions across town. Animals have living quarters, too. When you watch these creatures, try to be respectful of their space. Don't stand close to nesting birds, touch spider webs, or carry off rocks that serve as shelter.

▼ SIGNS OF LIFE

If you don't see any animals in your backyard, look for clues. Animals leave behind tracks in the snow or soil, scratched or gnawed trees, and the remains of a meal. A pile of moth wings may be a sign that bats have been around, feeding on these lively night creatures.

LIVING SPACE ▲

Animals live near food, water, and shelter. But they may not stay in the same place year-round. Canadian geese nest during the summer in the northern United States and as far north as the Arctic tundra. For the winter, they migrate south, as far as Mexico. You may see them flying in great V-shaped flocks, or staying for the season in your backyard—a great source for food.

NIGHT VIEW

To view animals at night, use a flashlight to look around bushes and trees, but cover it with red tape, so animals won't be startled. Most small animals cannot see red light.

Many moths fly at night and are prey to bats, frogs, and lizards.

◄ DAY DOERS

Daybreak is the best time to search for signs of wildlife. Night creatures are finishing up their work, and daytime animals are getting a jump-start. You may spy a lizard charging itself in the warmth of the sun.

61

BUZZING BACKYARD

Even the smallest patch of yard comes alive with the buzzing and chirping of insects as they fly about, crawl creepily, and simply hang out. These little critters are both pests and helpers to humans. What would a backyard be without them?

▲ CICADA CHORUS

The cicada has an amazing life cycle. Periodical cicadas live underground for 17 years as nymphs (the stage after hatching from eggs). When the whole population crawls above ground and becomes adults, they live for only a month, "singing," mating, and laying eggs. This buzzing chorus can be heard a mile away!

▲ PEST PATROL

Ladybird beetles, also known as ladybugs, provide pest relief to farmers and gardeners by preying on mealybugs, mites, and other plant-killing insects.

◄ OUT FOR BLOOD

Most people agree that mosquitoes are pests. But these bugs don't bite just to bother us. Although female mosquitoes eat nectar, they need blood to help their eggs develop. After drinking your blood, a female lays her eggs—up to 500 of them!

▲ FIDDLING FELLOWS

You may not have ever seen a katydid—the green, long-legged relative of the cricket—but, chances are, you've heard one on a hot summer night. To attract females, males rub a sharp file on one wing against a scraper on the other wing, like a violinist moving a bow over a string. The raspy sound is music to female katydids.

▲ BEE GOOD

Bees keep your backyard beautiful. Attracted to bright colors, bees land on flowers to feed on nectar. While they suck the sweet syrup, they pick up pollen grains and store them in baskets on their hind legs. Then they carry the grains to other flowers and pollinate them, causing the flowers to produce more seeds.

◄ FIERY FELLOW

Most ants are harmless, often crawling unnoticed between your toes as you sit in the backyard. But the red fire ant bites and injects venom, causing a burning sensation. This native of Brazil came to the United States in the 1930s, aboard ships. When they arrived, they multiplied and kept traveling.

▲ TWO-EYED TWIG

During the day, if you look closely in trees or shrubs, you just might spot a two-eyed twig! Stick insects avoid predators by sitting motionless. Usually long and thin, they are tree-green, leaf-brown, or any color that helps them blend into their background.

WINGED WONDERS

Your backyard is bursting with signs of bird life: baby-blue robins' eggs, nests of soft lichens, and spider webs. Birds big and small rustle about in treetops, so listen closely to their calls. You'll be surprised at how many different birds live in your own backyard!

EARLY BIRD ▼

Have you ever been the first to wake up? Probably not before the robin. As the sun rises, so does the robin, greeting the new day with its morning music, which sounds something like "cheer-up, cheer-up."

KNOCK, ▶ KNOCK!

That knocking you hear in the woods is probably a woodpecker. This tiny, downy bird climbs up trees using its stiff tail feathers and two pincerlike feet. With the help of its chisel-like bill, the bird chips away wood, then sticks out a long, slimy, barb-filled tongue, spearing its insect lunch.

HAWK HUNTERS ▶

The Cooper's hawk waits patiently to snare squirrels and other small animals. When food becomes scarce in the fall, these birds of prey fly south, often joining up with other species of hawks. Their mass migration over the Appalachian Mountains is one of the most spectacular sights to bird enthusiasts.

AQUA-BATICS
Go to a lake, and you may spot a grebe (GREEB). Grebes are great swimmers, gliding gracefully among reeds. When frightened, they sink quietly underwater, leaving just their neck and head above the surface.

TRAWLING FOR TRASH
Herring gulls, or seagulls, don't just chase ferries and hang out by the seashore. These scavengers feed at garbage dumps and in crowded cities. They also eat freshly caught mollusks, dropping them from high in the sky onto hard surfaces to crack open the shells.

▲ SWEET TREATS
As the hummingbird hovers above a brightly colored flower, it sips nectar at 13 licks per second. Its wings beat as fast as 78 times per second. These are the only birds that can fly backwards!

COOING COURTSHIP
The mourning dove gets its name from the male's sad "cooo, cooo." Actually, this call is an important part of courting. During courtship, the male soars high in the sky and then swoops down, making big, sweeping circles before returning to his perch beside the female.

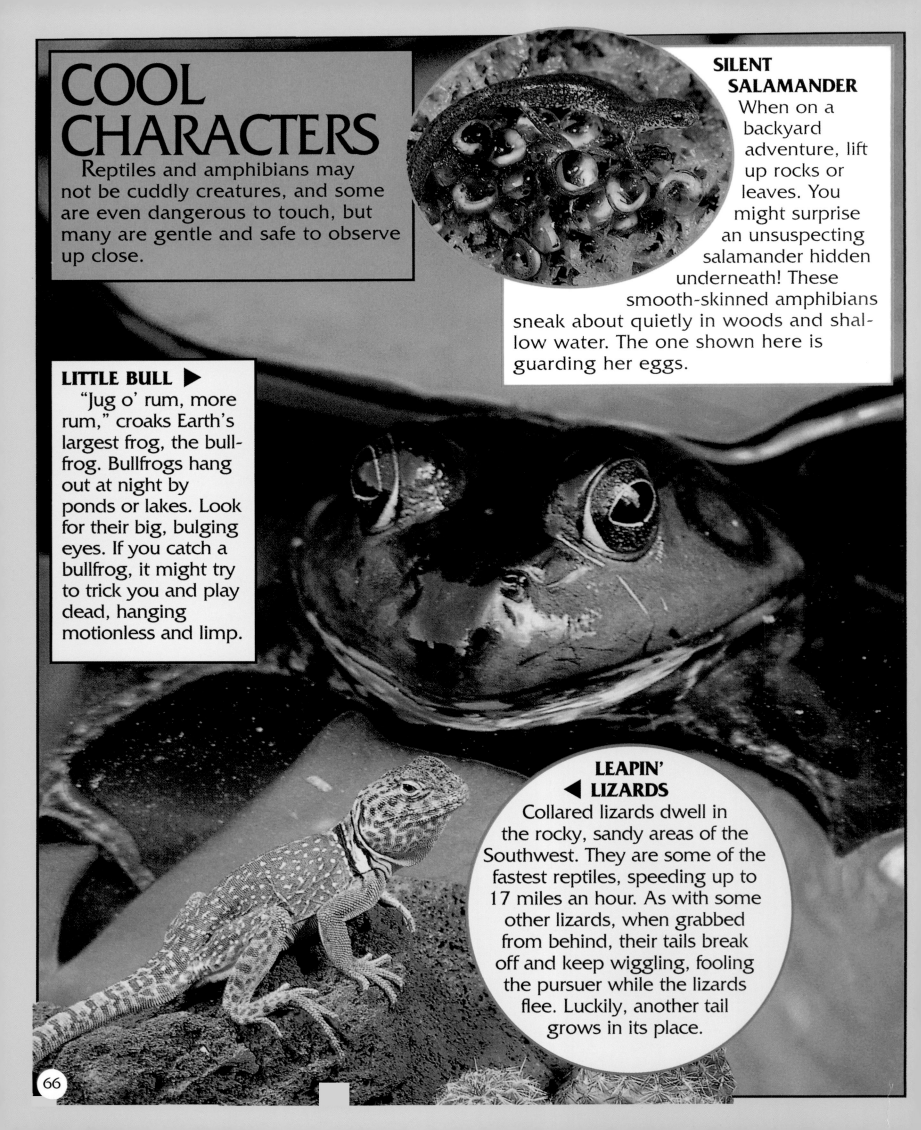

COOL CHARACTERS

Reptiles and amphibians may not be cuddly creatures, and some are even dangerous to touch, but many are gentle and safe to observe up close.

SILENT SALAMANDER

When on a backyard adventure, lift up rocks or leaves. You might surprise an unsuspecting salamander hidden underneath! These smooth-skinned amphibians sneak about quietly in woods and shallow water. The one shown here is guarding her eggs.

LITTLE BULL ▶

"Jug o' rum, more rum," croaks Earth's largest frog, the bullfrog. Bullfrogs hang out at night by ponds or lakes. Look for their big, bulging eyes. If you catch a bullfrog, it might try to trick you and play dead, hanging motionless and limp.

LEAPIN' ◀ LIZARDS

Collared lizards dwell in the rocky, sandy areas of the Southwest. They are some of the fastest reptiles, speeding up to 17 miles an hour. As with some other lizards, when grabbed from behind, their tails break off and keep wiggling, fooling the pursuer while the lizards flee. Luckily, another tail grows in its place.

◀ TOADS AMUCK!

Farmers brought the cane toad to Australia to eat cane beetles, which were eating up sugarcane roots. But now there's a bigger problem—millions of cane toads have spread all over the country, eating small mammals and infesting backyards.

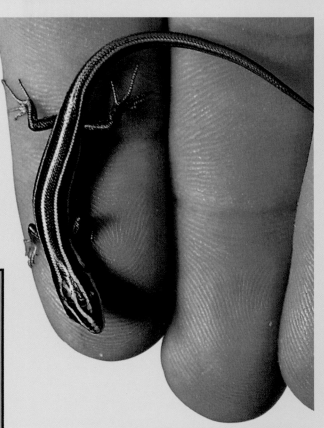

PEST PATROL

Slithering snakes seem scary, but they are important pest patrollers, feeding on rats and mice. This corn snake lives in woods, cornfields, plains, and in southern cities.

▲ SKINK HIJINKS

Skinks are teeny lizards that live near tree stumps or decaying driftwood. The male five-lined skink chooses a mate by nipping at the necks of other skinks. If a skink bites back, it's a male; but if it stays still or runs off, it's a female!

SNAPPY EATER

Snapping turtles like to bury themselves under mud at the bottom of creeks, awaiting their next meal—usually an unlucky fish. You might also see this warty-legged turtle prowling about on land in early summer, searching for a place to lay its eggs.

67

BEAUTY IN FLIGHT

Some of the most colorful, delicate animals in the back-yard, butterflies float from flower to flower in search of their next meal of nectar or pollen. Moths, their relatives, may not be as brightly colored, but that's because they mostly come out at night.

This swallowtail butterfly feeds on a sunflower.

A camouflaged green, the luna moth is amazing to see.

◀ WEIRD UP CLOSE

They may look pretty from a distance, but butterflies and moths look strange up close. They have a head, antennae, six legs, a body in three parts, scales, and thousands of eyes that allow them to see all around them at once.

THE FIRST CHANGES

The metamorphosis (meh-tuh-MORE-fuh-sus) of a caterpillar into a butterfly seems magical. Hatched from an egg, the caterpillar sheds its skin as it grows. Then it attaches itself to a twig with silk, and its skin forms a hardened shell called a *chrysalis*. Some moth caterpillars wrap themselves inside a silk case called a *cocoon*. After weeks, or even months, a butterfly or moth breaks out, dries itself, and takes off in search of food and a mate.

The cecropia moth

MONARCH MIGRATION

Butterflies and moths have a short life—some live for only a few days, others for as long as 10 months! Some that live through a change of seasons will migrate. In the fall, large monarch groups travel nearly 2,000 miles from the north to warmer climates in California and Mexico. They create quite a spectacle when they gather in trees to hibernate for the winter.

MAGIC DUST?

If a butterfly lights on your hand, be careful not to touch its wings. If you do, you'll find that a very fine dust rubs off on your skin. Although not dangerous to you, the loss of this dust could be bad for the butterfly, because it consists of the very small scales that cover the insect's body. Scales may be very plain or very colorful, or may form intricate designs on the wings.

The regal moth

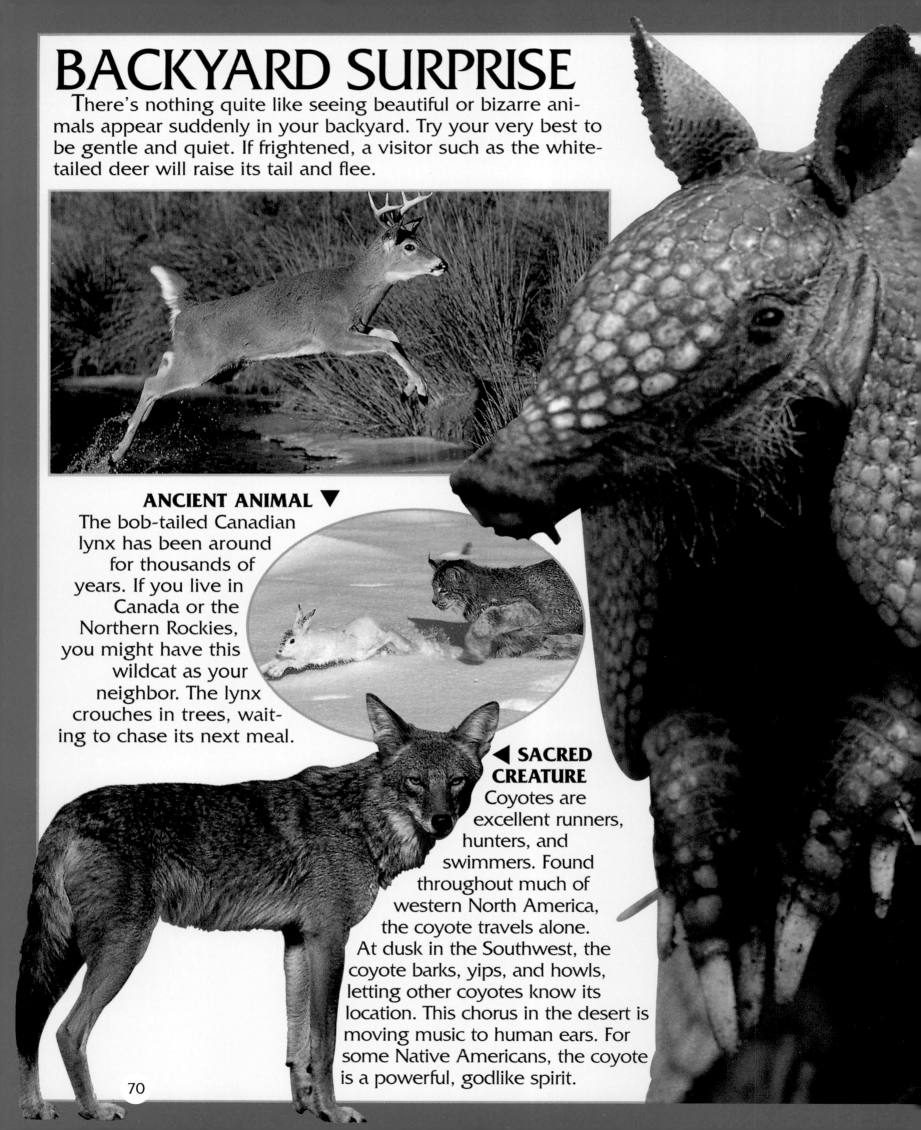

BACKYARD SURPRISE

There's nothing quite like seeing beautiful or bizarre animals appear suddenly in your backyard. Try your very best to be gentle and quiet. If frightened, a visitor such as the white-tailed deer will raise its tail and flee.

ANCIENT ANIMAL ▼

The bob-tailed Canadian lynx has been around for thousands of years. If you live in Canada or the Northern Rockies, you might have this wildcat as your neighbor. The lynx crouches in trees, waiting to chase its next meal.

◀ SACRED CREATURE

Coyotes are excellent runners, hunters, and swimmers. Found throughout much of western North America, the coyote travels alone. At dusk in the Southwest, the coyote barks, yips, and howls, letting other coyotes know its location. This chorus in the desert is moving music to human ears. For some Native Americans, the coyote is a powerful, godlike spirit.

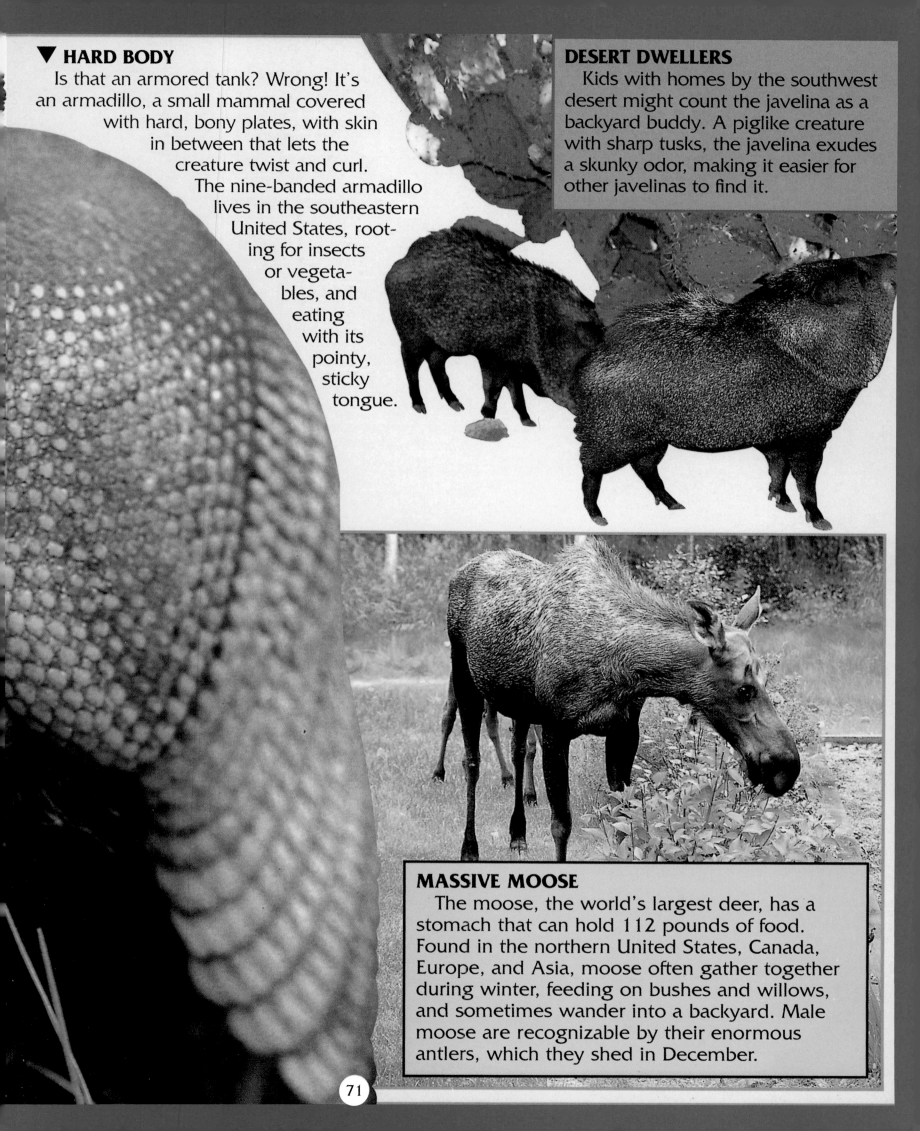

▼ HARD BODY

Is that an armored tank? Wrong! It's an armadillo, a small mammal covered with hard, bony plates, with skin in between that lets the creature twist and curl. The nine-banded armadillo lives in the southeastern United States, rooting for insects or vegetables, and eating with its pointy, sticky tongue.

DESERT DWELLERS

Kids with homes by the southwest desert might count the javelina as a backyard buddy. A piglike creature with sharp tusks, the javelina exudes a skunky odor, making it easier for other javelinas to find it.

MASSIVE MOOSE

The moose, the world's largest deer, has a stomach that can hold 112 pounds of food. Found in the northern United States, Canada, Europe, and Asia, moose often gather together during winter, feeding on bushes and willows, and sometimes wander into a backyard. Male moose are recognizable by their enormous antlers, which they shed in December.

FURRY FORAGERS

Even the critters you find cutest can do damage to your lawn, flower patch, or garden. Others might raid your garbage.

DIG THIS ▲

Badgers build elaborate habitats. Using sharp claws, they dig burrow systems, or setts, in forests or other sheltered areas. Badgers keep their homes really clean. Each sett has a separate area for sleeping, breeding, and even "going to the bathroom." Sometimes, badgers use the same home that their grandparents lived in!

HOP ALONG ▲

Cuddly cottontail rabbits may look cute, hopping around your yard. But they do something that you might think is disgusting—they eat their own droppings! Actually, the bunny is being healthy, because its body gets more nutrients when its food is digested twice.

BOXING BUNNIES

Hares are oversized rabbits, equipped with long ears, very thick fur, and strong hind legs that help them run up to 35 miles an hour and jump 6 1/2 feet high! Male brown hares have an interesting way of winning a female's affection. They play-fight another male, chasing, kicking, and "boxing," until one of them gives up.

WILY WEASELS ▼

Like many other mammals, weasels are carnivores. Sneaky hunters, weasels occasionally rob eggs, but a tasty mouse meal is always lip-smacking good to them. So a weasel near your house means one less mouse!

THE NOSE KNOWS

One of the funniest-looking creatures in the world lives only in North America, and maybe in your backyard! The star-nosed mole sports a "star nose," or ring of 22 pink, fleshy feelers. This ground habitant scrounges for food in ponds and on soil, its star nose moving about, feeling for insect larvae and earthworms.

EGG-CEPTIONAL

Echidnas, dwelling near Australian backyards, are spiny, ant-sucking creatures that have spellbound scientists for years. Although they are warm-blooded like mammals, they lay leathery eggs—like those of reptiles. Scientists created a whole new mammal category just for the echidna and its relative, the platypus.

▲ REAL STINKERS

When a skunk is startled, it stamps its feet, turns its back, and raises its tail—and out squirts a horrible, stinking liquid! Skunks can fire six rounds of this putrid juice. So if you spot a skunk toddling around, remain still, because the skunk may interpret your quick movements as threatening behavior.

GNAW-IT-ALLS

Rodents have large, sharp teeth—perfect for gnawing and cutting. These teeth are constantly growing. Rodents have to gnaw every day to keep them short. If you see chewed-up tree trunks, you know who the culprits are! But rodents also eat insects and weeds, improving the look of your yard and freeing it from pests.

BRILLIANT BUILDERS

At night, busy beavers gnaw on young trees, then haul, roll, or drag them downriver, their paddlelike tails helping them swim. Using stones, mud, and branches, these clever craftsmen construct dams, creating ponds where they build their dome-shaped lodge.

CHUBBY CHEEKS ▼

Chipmunks chatter, chirp, and whistle, but their high-pitched "chip-chip" gave them their name. Chipmunks spend their days stuffing their cheek pouches with seeds, nuts, and fruit. A chipmunk can hold up to four nuts in each chubby cheek pouch!

FATTENING UP ▼

Woodchucks, also known as groundhogs and whistle pigs, hibernate, or sleep, during winter. In summer months, they eat plenty of food, gorging themselves on plants and sometimes vegetables from your garden.

TALL TAILS

The gray squirrel has a big, bushy tail that helps it move, maintain balance, stay warm, and even communicate. When a squirrel senses an enemy, it flashes its tail to warn other squirrels. When a squirrel falls from a tree, the tail acts like a parachute. In the rain, the tail is an umbrella!

HOUSE MOUSE

Like its rat cousins, the house mouse will chew, suck, and eat almost anything, carefully clenching its meal in its front paw and gnawing with sharp front teeth. Mice love grains, but they'll also eat strings, paper, and even cable wire!

STICKY SITUATION ▲

The porcupine may be clumsy and slow, but it has an amazing way of protecting itself. When surprised, the porcupine will bristle up its 30,000 sharp spines, or long hairs, and slash its tail, sticking the enemy with the dangerous points. Porcupines love salt, and often gnaw on tools that have been held by sweaty palms.

Photo Credits

- iStock: Cover; End Pages (Front)
- PhotoDisc/Nature, Wildlife and the Environment 2: End Pages (Front and Back); pages 2-3
- Tom Bledsoe: page 9
- François Gohier: pages 10, 14-15, 20, 25, 31, 49, 51, 54, 57, 61
- Glen & Rebecca L. Grambo: pages 4, 7, 8, 16
- Larry Kimball: page 8
- Dwight Kuhn: pages 10, 11, 17, 60-61, 63, 68, 73, 75
- Tom & Pat Leeson: pages 5, 9, 11-12, 16, 18-19, 33, 37, 44, 48, 53, 56, 64, 70, 74-75
- Kevin Schafer: pages 5 - 7, 10, 15
- Kevin Schafer & Martha Hill: page 13
- Merlin Tuttle: page 17
- Art Wolfe: pages 7, 16, 18, 20, 22, 48-49, 56, 60
- Norbert Wu: page 12
- Gavriel Jecan/Art Wolfe Inc.: page 14
- Tom Brakefield/DRK: pages 8, 14
- J. Cancalosi/DRK: pages 8, 65, 73
- John Gerlach/DRK: pages 4, 51, 59
- Johnny Johnson/DRK: pages 11, 49-51, 57-58, 61
- Steven Kaufman/DRK: pages 6, 46
- Stephen J. Krasemann/DRK: pages 18, 63
- Wayne Lynch/DRK: pages 19, 48, 52-53
- Joe McDonald/DRK: page 4
- David Woodfall/DRK: page 6
- Belinda Wright/DRK: page 17
- Gerry Ellis: ENP Images: pages 9, 11, 13, 20, 23-25, 28-29, 30, 32, 35, 38
- Peter Howorth/Mo Yung Productions: page 5
- John D. Cunningham/Visuals Unlimited: pages 18-19
- David B. Fleetham/Visuals Unlimited: page 12
- Rod Kieft/Visuals Unlimited: page 13
- Ken Lucas/Visuals Unlimited: page 14, 24, 28, 38-39, 47, 69
- Joe McDonald/Visuals Unlimited: page 9
- R. A. Simpson/Visuals Unlimited: page 15
- Gary Walter/Visuals Unlimited: page 19
- Stephen Frink/Waterhouse: page 13
- Michael Francis/Wildlife Collection: page 18
- Martin Harvey/ Wildlife Collection: pages 4, 25, 30, 32, 34, 44
- Bob Jacobson: page 22
- Zig Leszczynski: pages 20, 34-35, 66, 72, 74
- Mark Newman: pages 31, 36
- Michael Durham/ENP: page 22
- Pete Oxford/ENP: page 24
- Terry Whittaker/ENP: page 24,
- Konrad Wothe/ENP: pages 36, 38
- Kenfre Inc./International Stock: page 29
- Phillip Little/International Stock: page 29
- A.J. Copley/Visuals Unlimited: page 20
- Tom DiMauro/Wildlife Collection: pages 23, 33
- Tim Laman/Wildlife Collection: pages 32, 67
- Dean Lee/Wildlife Collection: pages 39, 56-57
- Jack Swenson/Wildlife Collection: pages 20, 33
- iStock: page 31
- Kit Kittle: page 41
- K. H. Switik/Photo Researchers: page 41
- Nathan W. Cohen/Visuals Unlimited: page 40
- Don W. Fawcett/Visuals Unlimited: page 41
- Jim Merli/Visuals Unlimited: page 40
- Joyce Photographics/Photo Researchers: page 41
- Rod Canham/WaterHouse: page 41
- Lynn Rogers: pages 42-43
- Anita Baskin-Salzberg: page 42
- Allen Salzberg: page 42
- Tom McHugh/Photo Researchers: pages 42-43
- W. Perry Conway: page 44
- Lynn M. Stone: pages 44, 57, 63
- M. P. Kahl/DRK: pages 45, 49-50
- S. Nielsen/DRK: pages 46-48
- George J. Sanker/DRK: page 45
- John Winnie, Jr./DRK: page 47
- S. Maslowski/Visuals Unlimited: pages 44, 74
- Library Services/AMNH Neg. No. 314878/Photo. Julius Kirschner: page 52
- John Eastcott/DRK: page 48
- Barbara Gerlach/DRK: page 59
- Annie Griffiths/DRK: page 58
- Ford Kristo (Australia)/DRK: page 51
- Leonard Lee Rue III/DRK: page 58
- N. Pecnik/Visuals Unlimited: page 58
- Brian Rogers/Visuals Unlimited: page 59
- Kjell B. Sandved/Visuals Unlimited: pages 48, 50, 55, 56, 60
- Tom Vezo/Wildlife Collection: pages 48-49, 55
- H. Rappel/Wildlife Collection: page 52
- Chris Huss/Wildlife Collection: pages 53-54
- Stefan Lundgren/Wildlife Collection: page 59
- Dennis Frieborn/Wildlife Collection: page 58
- R. E. Barber: pages 60, 71-73
- Bill Beatty: page 64
- Rick & Nora Bowers: page 65
- Cathy & Gordon Illg: pages 61, 70, 72
- Breck P. Kent: pages 66, 69
- A. B. Sheldon: pages 67, 69
- Gary Vestal: page 68
- Marty Cordano/DRK: page 60
- R. J. Erwin/DRK: pages 62-63
- Jeff Foott/DRK: page 62
- Wayne Lankinen/DRK: page 65
- Buddy Mays/International Stock: page 61
- S. Myers/International Stock: page 72
- Callahan/Visuals Unlimited: page 62
- Jeffrey Howe/Visuals Unlimited: page 67
- J. L. McAlonan/Visuals Unlimited: page 65
- Glenn M. Oliver/Visuals Unlimited: page 71
- Rob Simpson/Visuals Unlimited: page 75
- Richard Walters/Visuals Unlimited: page 62
- W. J. Weber/Visuals Unlimited: page 63
- Ken Deitcher/The Wildlife Collection: page 69
- Henry Holdsworth/The Wildlife Collection: pages 70-71

Illustrations:
- Crystal Palette: page 43